lightweight **littermates**

sharon montrose

Stewart, Tabori & Chang

New York

Portions of this book were originally published in four separate editions:

Lightweights Littermates: French Bulldogs
Lightweights Littermates: Dachshunds
Lightweights Littermates: Poodles
Lightweights Littermates: Labs

Published in 2009 by Barnes & Noble, Inc., by arrangement with ABRAMS.

ISBN 978-1-4351-1800-3

Printed and bound in China.

10 9 8 7 6 5 4 3 2 1

stewart tabori & chang
An imprint of Harry N. Abrams, Inc.
115 West 18th Street
New York, NY 10011
www.stcbooks.com

lightweight **littermates** six weeks old

tabitha 5 lbs. 8 ozs.

peter **5** lbs. **14** ozs.

mitts 5 lbs. 3 ozs.

arrow **5** lbs. 12 ozs.

nick **5** lbs. **11** ozs.

angelus **6** lbs. 1oz.

ashley **5** lbs. **6** ozs.

lightweight **littermates** four weeks old

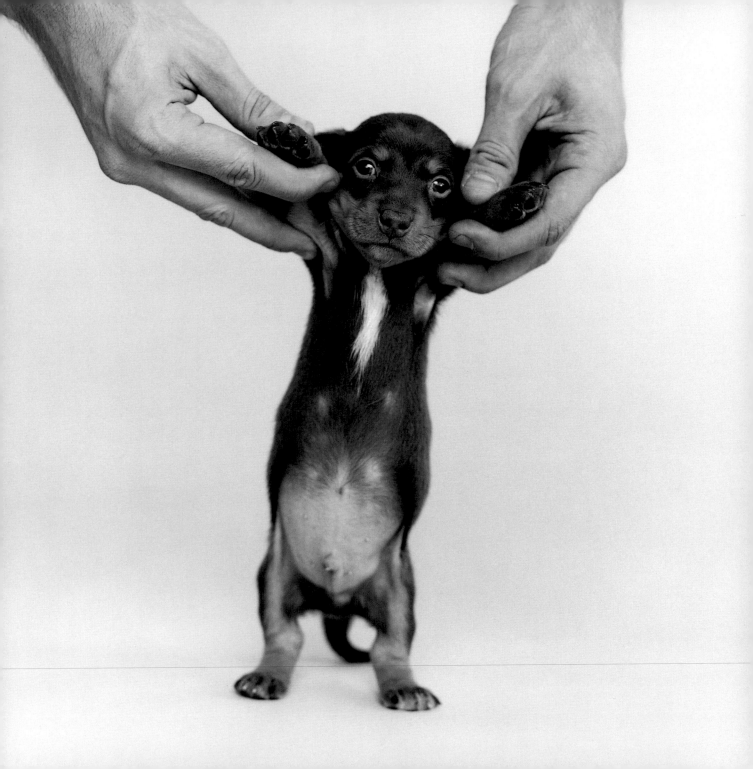

brownie 2 lbs. 6 ozs.

fozzy **2** lbs. 4 ozs.

beatrice **2** lbs. 4 ozs.

poke **2** lbs. **5** ozs.

lightweight **littermates** eight weeks old

ronnie O lbs. 15 ozs.

reginald O lbs. 14 ozs.

lightweight **littermates** five weeks old

harpo 4 lbs, 8 ozs.

chico 4lbs. 3ozs.

groucho 3lbs. 15ozs.

zeppo 4lbs. 13ozs.

vera 3lbs. 6ozs.

lightweight littermates eight weeks old

mirna **7** lbs. **13** ozs.

clark **8** lbs. **4** ozs.

alfred **9** lbs. **2** ozs.

vivian **8** lbs. **8** ozs.

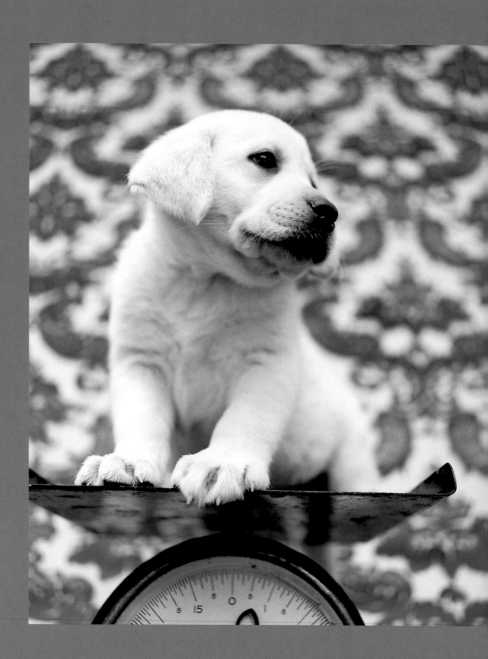

chaplin 8 lbs. 13 ozs.

jane **8** lbs. **6** ozs.

hardy **9** lbs. **4** ozs.

bishop **9** lbs. **2** ozs.

slim **8**lbs.1oz.

lightweight **littermates** four weeks old

branford 2 lbs. 4 ozs.

wynton 2 lbs. 2 ozs.

lightweight **littermates**

flyboy 4 lbs. 13 ozs.

loretta 4 lbs. 5 ozs.

lightweight **littermates** four weeks old

bouy 1 lb. 2 ozs.

leopold **1** lb.**4**ozs.

millie **1** lb. **3** ozs.

gretta **1** lb. **1**oz.

lightweight **littermates** seven weeks old

cocoa 6 lbs. 3 ozs.

shy 5 lbs. 15 ozs.

willy 5 lbs. 2 ozs.

roger **6** lbs. **8** ozs.

cur 5 lbs. 11 ozs.

calvin 6 lbs. 8 ozs.

godiva 5 lbs. 8 ozs.

hershey **6** lbs. **9** ozs.

lightweight **littermates** seven weeks old

claudine 1 lb. 8 ozs.

pascal 2 lbs. 0 ozs.

lightweight **littermates** seven weeks old

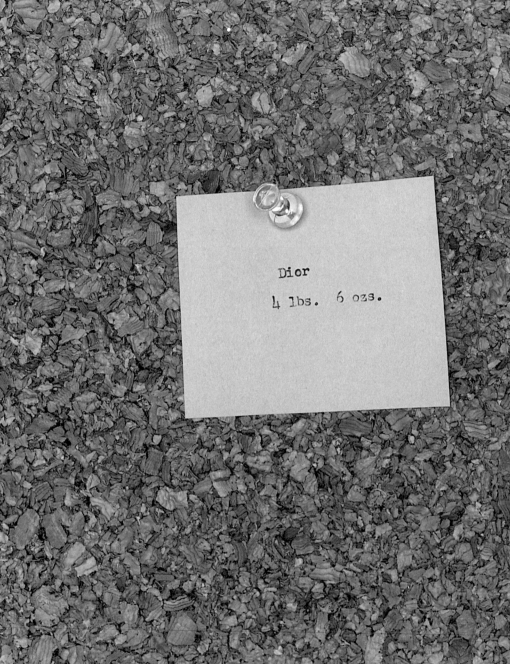

Dior

4 lbs. 6 ozs.

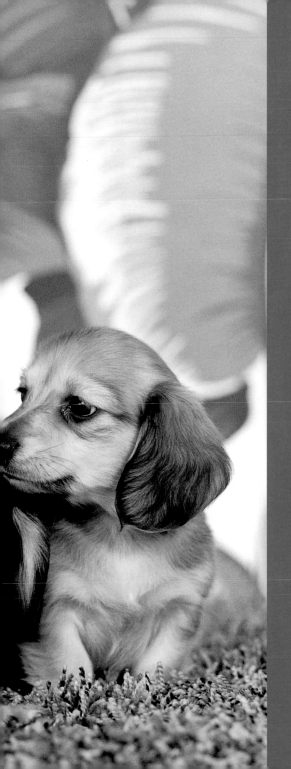

lightweight **littermates** five weeks old

basie **1** lb. **6** ozs.

bird **1** lb. **8** ozs.

vaughn **1** **lb.** **7** ozs.

dexter **1** lb. **5** ozs.

ella **1** lb. **3** ozs.

mercer **1** lb. **1** oz.

lightweight **litterm**

duchess 2 lbs. 15 ozs.

empress 3 lbs. 3 ozs.

marie 3 lbs. 6 ozs.

archduke 3 lbs. 7 ozs.

lightweight **littermates** six weeks old

henderson 3 lbs. 2 ozs.

maybelle 2 lbs. 1 oz.

june 3 lbs. 5 ozs.

johnny **1** lb. **7** ozs.

rozanna 3 lbs. 4 ozs.

carlene 3 lbs. 6 ozs.

lightweight **littermates** five weeks old

speck **1** lb. 3ozs.

mole **1** lb. **8** ozs.

djuna 1 lb. 5 ozs.

bing 1 lb. 5 ozs.

cola 1 lb. 6 ozs.

MADELINE PATTERSON

SUSANA LABRADORS www.susanalabradors.com

NORMA B. THOMPSON www.parti-poodles.com

TRACEY ALBERRI www.californialabs.com

NORMA B. THOMPSON www.parti-poodles.com

SUSANA LABRADORS www.susanalabradors.com

LISA KENDRICK http://bullyrat.tripod.com

all dachshunds **provided by:** Stone Family Dachshunds 949-364-0336
www.stonesfamilydachshunds.com

LINDA MAUGERI www.geocities.com/lindamaugeri

AIMEE MARSH

LISA KENDRICK http://bullyrat.tripod.com

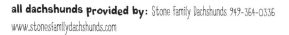